KT-146-275

focus on
NEW YORK

◆ *inspiring places, beautiful spaces* ◆

Written by Donna Dailey
Designed by Jeremy Tilston of The Oak Studio Limited
Produced by AA Publishing
Text © Automobile Association Developments Limited 2007
For details of photograph copyrights see page 96

All rights reserved. No part of this publication may be
reproduced, stored in a retrieval system, or transmitted in any
form or by any means – electronic, photocopying, recording
or otherwise – unless the written permission of the publisher
has been obtained beforehand.

Published by AA Publishing (a trading name of Automobile
Association Developments Limited, whose registered office
is Fanum House, Basing View, Basingstoke, Hampshire
RG21 4EA; registered number 1878835).

A03202

ISBN-10: 0-7495-5208-5
ISBN-13: 978-0-7495-5208-4

A CIP catalogue record for this book is available
from the British Library.

Colour reproduction by KDP, Kingsclere, England
Printed in China by C&C Offset Printing

PICTURES FROM TOP TO BOTTOM:
The Stars and Stripes hang from the bastion of the country's
commerce, the New York Stock Exchange.

Vendors sell hot pretzels on street corners throughout the city.

Times Square is the pulsating heart of Manhattan.

PAGE 3: the Statue of Liberty in New York Harbor is a symbol
of hope and freedom around the world.

PAGE 4: bright lights emanate from Radio City Music Hall at
Rockefeller Center. Built in 1932, this art-deco gem was then
the largest theater in the world and is now a National
Historic Landmark.

focus on
NEW YORK

◆ *inspiring places, beautiful spaces* ◆

INTRODUCTION

No other city in America compares with New York. Whether you see it as the Big Apple, the Empire City, or Gotham – just a few of the nicknames it has acquired over the years – it looms so large in the public imagination that it's in a league of its own. What sets New York apart is its nonstop energy, which pulsates out to the rest of the world in finance, fashion, art, and entertainment.

From its origins as a Dutch fur-trading post in the early 1600s, New York went on to become an English colony, a prosperous seaport, and a gateway to the New World for millions of immigrants. Today it is the largest city in the United States. Its population numbers over eight million, embracing a rainbow of faces, languages, and ethnic groups from almost every country around the globe. From stockbrokers to taxi drivers to restaurant owners to office workers, their lives and labors fuel the powerhouse of this great metropolis.

Although New York is comprised of five boroughs, including Brooklyn, Queens, the Bronx, and Staten Island, Manhattan is its heart and soul, the vortex of mass and motion around which everything revolves. Bordered by the East and Hudson rivers, with the Harlem River to the north and Upper New York Bay to the south, this long, narrow island is only 13$\frac{1}{2}$ miles long and 2$\frac{1}{4}$ miles wide. Yet despite its international outlook, New Yorkers have their own island mentality: those who are smitten by its charms say they could never live anywhere else.

Many of the elements that make New York such a dazzling, effervescent place are shown on the following pages, from the bright lights of Radio City Music Hall and the neon billboards of Times Square to the soaring glass-walled skyscrapers that reflect the sky. The flash of yellow cabs in the night, curious Chinese herbs and spices, hot pretzels sizzling in a street vendor's cart, or the twinkling night lights from its great suspension bridges mirrored in the river are pictures that linger in the mind long after a visit to the city.

There are surprising images, too, for such a cosmopolitan city. These urban views are not all concrete, stone, and steel. The vast, green lung of Central Park is criss-crossed by woodland and rambling streams, sunny lakes, and shady paths. There are quiet cloisters and blossoming gardens. Scenes of everyday life, from a patriotic mailbox to a baseball game, could be found as readily in any small town as in the nation's largest city. New York is a patriotic city, and the Stars and Stripes adorn the facades of department stores, businesses, and public buildings. And while New York is always changing, tearing down the old to make way for the new, you can still find remnants of its roots in historic churches and buildings that date back to the 17th century.

Above all (literally), there are the skyscrapers. Though it wasn't invented here, the skyscraper became an art form in New York as 20th-century developers raced to build them ever higher. The result is one of the world's most remarkable skylines. In fact, New York skyscrapers are much like its people: crowded together, reaching for the heights, each with its own style and personality. Some are topped by pyramids, others are art deco masterpieces inside and out. Some are incredibly ornate, others sleek and minimalist. Closer to the ground are more of the most acclaimed buildings in the country, from the Beaux Arts glory of Grand Central Terminal to the spiraling genius of the Guggenheim Museum of Art.

Two skyscrapers have become much-loved symbols of the city. The Empire State Building, at 1,454 feet (102 stories) high, is the tallest building in the city. The views from its observation deck are unforgettable. With its gleaming stainless-steel spire and automotive motifs, the Chrysler Building was both brilliant and daring for its time, a symbol of New York's – and America's – wealth, power, and innovation. Other New York images have become national icons, most notably the Statue of Liberty, which stands on an island in New York Harbor, raising her torch as a sign of welcome and refuge to all who the USA.

Amid the great structure of their city, New Yorkers are always on the move. Whether on foot, bicycle, or by bus, in a taxi, subway car, or commuter train, there is a constant ebb and flow between Uptown and Downtown, across the bridges and through the tunnels, of people at work or at leisure, pumping the life blood through the city's arteries. This movement goes on round the clock, giving New York another nickname: the City that Never Sleeps. At any hour, New York is one of the most vibrant places on the planet: often beautiful, never dull, always inspiring.

Opposite: the Alma Mater statue by Daniel Chester French spreads her arms as if to welcome all to the land of learning at Columbia University. She graces the steps of the Low Memorial Library, designed in 1897 by Charles McKim to resemble the classical buildings of Rome.

The handsome townhouses surrounding Gramercy Park are remnants
of the genteel residential squares that were built in Lower Midtown in
the mid-19th century. They were designed by top architects, such as
Stanford White, who had a home here himself, alongside the homes of
other leading politicians and actors of the day.

Pages 6–7: New York is the city that never sleeps. With a 24-hour
subway and taxis plying the popular routes between Uptown and
Downtown, nightlife literally lasts all night, from sunset to sunrise.

In the early 20th century, the streets of Little Italy teemed with immigrants from the old country.
Their legacy is the cluster of authentic Italian restaurants and delis that flourish here today.
Opposite: New York's largest greenmarket (or farmers' market) is held several days a week in Union
Square. City chefs and foodies flock here for everything from honey and cheese to a variety of chili peppers.

Lower Manhattan's Chinatown is the largest in the country. This is the place to find herbal remedies, pungent spices and Far Eastern foodstuffs, as well as hundreds of Chinese restaurants.
Opposite: a spider's web of steel cables and wires supports the Brooklyn Bridge. It was the world's first suspension bridge built of steel and was completed in 1883. It is anchored on either side by Gothic double-arched towers, which stand 277 feet high.

Even in the busy metropolis, New Yorkers can get away from it all with a boat ride on The Lake in Central Park, rowing beneath the cast-iron arch of pretty Bow Bridge.

A statue of George Washington looks out on the New York Stock Exchange, now a center of world finance. In his day, the nation's first brokers sealed their deals here under a buttonwood tree.

Despite its size, New York is very much a walking city. Walking is a great way to avoid traffic jams,
to people-watch, to admire the architecture – and it's New Yorkers' secret to staying slim.
Opposite: a gift from France, the Statue of Liberty was unveiled in 1886 and stands on Liberty Island in
New York Harbor. She holds her torch aloft as a symbol of welcome and refuge for visitors and immigrants
from across the globe.
Pages 16–17: from the Empire State Building's observation deck, the facades of the Midtown district form a
striking architectural patchwork of shapes and sizes. Each year 4 million visitors enjoy this view.

Manhattan is an island, and the best place to see its famous skyline is from offshore. The Circle Line
sightseeing boats cruise the waters around its shoreline, taking in all the major landmarks.
Opposite: inside and out, the Empire State Building is one of New York's great art deco masterpieces.
The Fifth Avenue lobby features marble walls, one of which depicts the building in brilliant metal relief.
Pages 20–21: with its retro decor of chrome, black, and stainless steel bar, the Empire Diner is a 1920s
American classic but still pulls in the fashionable Chelsea clubbing crowd with its round-the-clock service.

A spot of sunlight reaches between the buildings to illuminate the southern side of Grand Army Plaza.
This semi-circular plaza borders Fifth Avenue and forms the main, southeast gateway to Central Park.

New York's yellow cabs are so well known they've become a city icon. The first ones hit the streets in 1907, and today more than 12,000 taxis ferry passengers around the metropolitan area.

New York's top hotels offer every possible amenity, from luxurious rooms with views of the Statue of Liberty to opulent lobbies and fine dining. Service with a smile is part of the hospitality.
Opposite: At Christmas, shopping streets and large stores, such as Macy's, are adorned with festive lights. Even the Empire State Building displays the holiday spirit with colorful floodlights.

The Cloisters in Fort Tryon Park, at the northern tip of Manhattan in Washington Heights, was reassembled from real medieval monastic cloisters brought from Spain and southern France. It is home to the Metropolitan Museum of Art's medieval collection.

An ornamental sculpture featuring, appropriately, Mercury, the Roman god of travel and commerce, crowns the 42nd Street entrance to Grand Central Terminal. Hulking over this beaux arts landmark is the incongruous modern MetLife Building.

Rising 330 feet above Fifth Avenue, the twin spires of St. Patrick's Cathedral were once among the tallest structures in Midtown. Now they are dwarfed by the surrounding skyscrapers. Opposite: baseball is New York's favorite sport. When the weather is fine, young players like this one in Central Park don their helmets, raise their bats, and enjoy the thrill of the game. Pages 30–31: the George Washington Bridge spans the Hudson River, connecting upper Manhattan with New Jersey. With more than 105 million vehicles crossing it annually, it is said to be the busiest bridge in the world.

The graceful wrought-iron railings and red-brick facade of the Chelsea Hotel belie its notoriety. Well-known literary residents here included Mark Twain, Eugene O'Neill, and Jack Kerouac, and the hotel featured in Andy Warhol's 1966 movie, Chelsea Girls.

In its heyday in the early 1900s, Time Square was often called the 'Crossroads of the World.' In recent
years it has reclaimed its legacy as the city's brightest hub for entertainment, with around 1.5 million
people passing through the square every day.

Affectionately known as 'Bloomie's,' the Midtown department store founded by the Bloomingdale brothers in 1872 is a much-loved New York institution, always well-stocked with the latest fashions.
Opposite: Times Square is a public gathering place, particularly on New Year's Eve. Millions of Americans join in via their television sets to count down the seconds to midnight as a glowing ball drops down a pole on the roof of the 25-story Times Tower.

Though Manhattan can sometimes seem like a huge concrete jungle, New Yorkers can always find a spot of green and a breath of fresh air in the city's parks and squares.

Opposite: some of the biggest, brightest images of America's lifestyle are polished in New York, which is home to many of the world's top advertising agencies. They culminate in dozens of supersigns, such as this giant Coca-Cola bottle, in Duffy Square.

Pages 38–39: a patriotic row of Stars and Stripes dresses up the facade of Saks, the famous Fifth Avenue department store, which has been selling high-quality clothing and other goods here since 1924.

Paintings in the Guggenheim Museum are displayed along a six-story ramp which spirals upwards around the atrium in widening levels, like a Nautilus shell, to a huge domed skylight.
Opposite: floodlights illuminate the top 30 floors of the Empire State Building at night. The lights change color in honour of national holidays, seasons, special events, and the many ethnic groups living in New York. They are turned off during spring and fall bird migrations to protect the birds.
Pages 42–43: the Hudson River brought the city early sources of wealth from upstate New York. It prospered first as a fur-trading post under the Dutch and then later as a port for both agricultural produce and manufactured goods.

Outside Manhattan, the city streets give way to the residential neighborhoods of suburban New York.
A patriotic mailbox painted in the pattern of the American flag graces a home in the outer boroughs.
Opposite: parts of Central Park are more rural than urban. Trails and streams meander through the wild,
wooded area of the Ramble, which covers 37 acres and is a haven for birds and other wildlife.

Proudly known as 'New York's Finest,' some 35,000 officers are on the force of the New York City Police Department, which is the largest in the United States. They preserve the peace and enforce the laws in all five boroughs of the city, Manhattan, Brooklyn, Queens, the Bronx, and New Jersey.
Opposite: six major bridges and four tunnels connect Manhattan to the city's other boroughs.

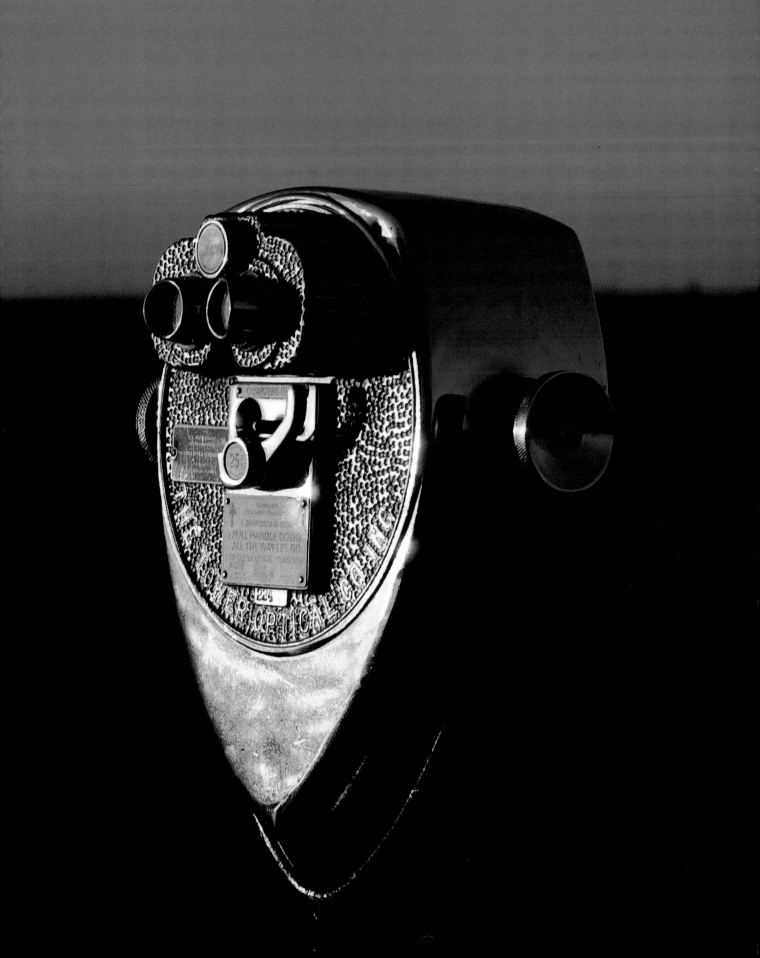

The luxury apartment buildings of the Upper West Side are reflected in the lake in Central Park, including
the twin-towered San Remo and the famous Dakota, where Beatle John Lennon was murdered in 1980.
Pages 50–51: the views over New York Harbor are magnificent, especially at sunrise and sunset.
Coin-operated look-outs in Battery Park provide close-up views of the Statue of Liberty.

The Cuxa Cloister is a beautiful example of 12th-century Romanesque architecture, transported here from Europe and reconstructed in the 1930s. It encloses the tranquil gardens of the Cloisters in Fort Tryon Park.

Plump, chewy New York bagels can't be beat. Which bagel shop is best is a subject for fierce debate, and some bagel bakers even export their wares to connoisseurs all over the world.
Opposite: books are another passion in this literary capital. Specialist bookstores range from history to mystery, and you can find great bargains at markets and second-hand bookstores, such as this one on Avenue A in the East Village.

It's generally easy to find a taxi in New York. Official taxicabs are always yellow, you can hail them in the street, and the rates are clearly displayed on the door.
Opposite: the Flatiron Building, given this nickname due to its distinctive and unusual shape, is one of the best-loved buildings in the city. The 20-story skyscraper was built in 1902 to fit a triangular plot of land at the crossing of Fifth Avenue and Broadway.
Pages 56–57: architect Frank Lloyd Wright's innovative circular design for the Guggenheim Museum is as impressive today as when it was first opened in 1959. The Guggenheim is his only New York building.

As the early skyscrapers in the Financial District rose ever higher, they created concrete canyons that kept pedestrians in perpetual shadow. Now buildings are designed to let sunlight and air reach the streets below.

Lincoln Center is the shining star of New York's performing arts scene. Three top venues surround its central plaza fountains: the Metropolitan Opera House, the New York State Theater, and Avery Fisher Hall, home to the New York Philharmonic Orchestra.

Union Square once anchored the southern end of the 19th-century shopping stretch known as Ladies'
Mile. Today it's a bustling meeting place, with a market and around 100 restaurants in the area.
Opposite: when it opened in 1877, the Jefferson Market Courthouse was voted the fifth most beautiful
building in the country. The building is now a public library and its Victorian Gothic tower and facade form
a landmark in Greenwich Village.

St. Mark's in the Bowery, which was built in 1660, is the oldest church in continual use in New York. It was built on the farm, or bouwerie, of the city's Dutch governor, Peter Stuyvesant, who is buried in the churchyard.

Opposite: a 50-foot tall Barosaurus greets visitors in the entrance hall of the American Museum of Natural History. The dinosaur halls, with an amazing collection of skeletons, are the museum's star attraction.

Visitors of all ages love New York. As is befitting a city known for its quick-witted patter and sense of humor, there is a range of wacky and tacky souvenirs.
Opposite: several generations of skyscrapers pose for a family portrait in Lower Manhattan. Topped by a green pyramid, 40 Wall Street opened in 1930, having lost its race to become New York's tallest skyscraper by 105 feet to the Chrysler Building.

Throughout New York, fire escapes are a distinctive part of the residential architecture, forming interesting
shapes and patterns on the facades of apartment buildings like these in Soho.
Opposite: fire has always been a serious hazard in a crowded city, but for children in the inner city,
a gushing fire hydrant is great way to cool off in the intense summer heat.

At the end of Wall Street, historic Trinity Church has a striking spire and a lovely interior with stained-glass windows and Gothic arches. Classical music concerts take place here on Thursday afternoons. Opposite: nearly one quarter of the city's population is under 18 years old. New York City's fleet of 6,200 yellow school buses is by far the largest in the country and takes 185,000 children to school.

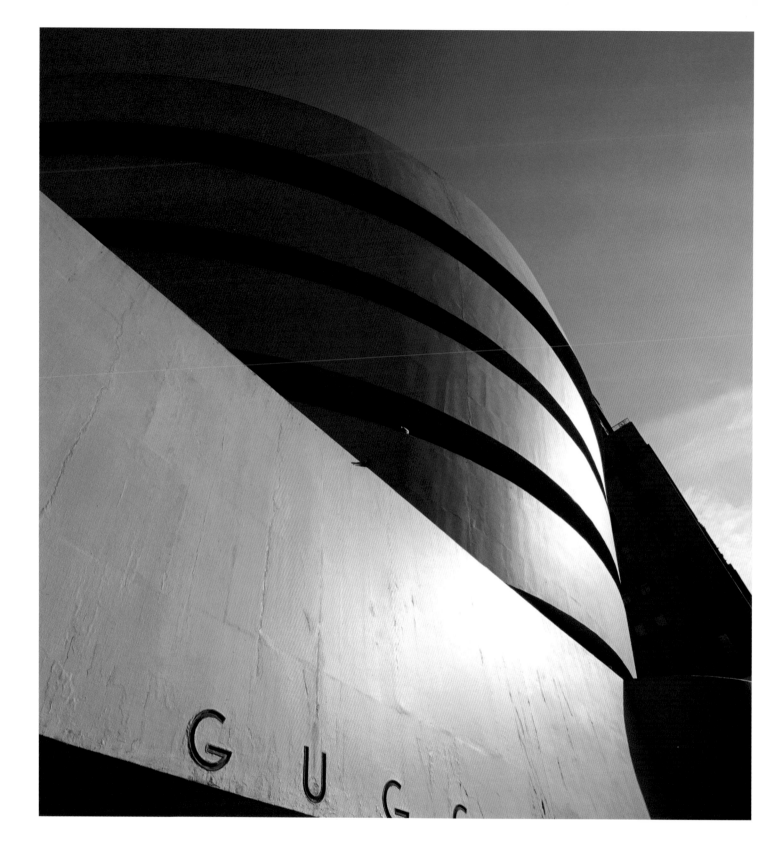

There's no excuse for being late! The four-faced brass clock above the information booth on the main concourse of Grand Central Terminal shows the time to all directions. Opposite: Solomon R. Guggenheim began collecting modern and contemporary art at the age of 66. Sadly, he died in 1949, and so never saw the magnificent building which was destined to display his collection.

From across the lake in Central Park, the view of the Midtown Manhattan skyline evokes a totally different mood at night, with the light from skyscraper windows emitting a futuristic glow.
Pages 74–75: completed in 1909, the Manhattan Bridge was the last of the three great suspension bridges constructed across the East River. Here, the reflections from its night lights shimmer in the water.

Cherry blossoms flutter through the springtime air in the Brooklyn Botanic Gardens. With more than 13,000 species of plants from around the world, this is one of the best spaces in the city for a green retreat.

Many people will recognize the lobby of the Daily News *building, with its giant revolving globe, from the classic* Superman *movies. The art deco facade over the front entrance is illuminated with neon at night. Opposite: in ultra-modern New York, where buildings are torn down and new ones go up almost every week, some people still cherish the past, such as at this second-hand store in SoHo. Pages 78–79: with its great arched windows, grand staircase, marble floor, and vaulted ceiling with zodiac constellations, Grand Central Terminal is a beaux arts gem. Every day, around half a million commuters move through its main concourse.*

A fresh catch arrives at South Street Seaport's Fulton Fish Market every day before dawn. By lunchtime, it's on the menu at seafood restaurants across the city, such as this one in Chelsea.

Pages 80–81: New York's characters and cityscapes have always been a source of inspiration for writers, artists, and musicians. Its glass-walled skyscrapers provide endless opportunities for creative photography.

Created in the mid-19th century, Central Park was the first artificially landscaped park in the country.
Its bridges, boating lakes, bridle paths and miles of footpaths give New Yorkers a place to relax.

New Yorkers are always on the go, but here fast food is a culinary art, from freshly baked bagels and hot dogs with 'the works' to noodle bars on wheels and real Italian pizza by the slice.

Opposite: the gleaming, stainless steel spire of the Chrysler Building was designed to look like the radiator grill of a car. The art deco building, which was erected in 1929, is a much-loved symbol of the city.

Pages 86–87: this striking sculpture in SoHo is a monument to the workers who braved the heights to build the city's skyscrapers. The construction of the Empire State Building alone took 7 million man hours.

The original Cotton Club in Harlem was one of New York's most famous nightclubs, where Duke Ellington, Cab Calloway, Louis Armstrong, and the jazz greats of the 1920s and '30s once played.

Times Square displayed the world's first running electrical sign in 1928. Today, dozens of brilliant, animated, neon mega-signs illuminate buildings around the square, as required by local zoning laws!

Whatever your heart desires can be found somewhere in New York's plethora of fashion emporiums, funky boutiques, jewelers, toy stores, specialty stores and more.

Opposite: in the 1880s, Times Square became the center of New York's theater district, collectively known as 'Broadway,' and has remained so to this day. Now movie theaters and TV studios round out this entertainment hub.

Pages 92–93: within the great expanse of Central Park there are 58 miles of paths for jogging and cycling. At weekends, it's full of fitness-conscious New Yorkers, who welcome the chance to tone their figure.

INDEX

ACKNOWLEDGMENTS

The Automobile Association would like to thank the following photographers, companies and picture libraries for their assistance in the preparation of this book.

Abbreviations for the picture credits are as follows: - (t) top; (b) bottom; (l) left; (r) right; (AA) AA World Travel Library.
2t AA/C Sawyer; 2c AA/C Sawyer; 2b AA/C Sawyer; 3 AA/C Sawyer; 4 AA/C Sawyer; 6/7 AA/C Sawyer; 8/9 AA/R Elliot; 9 AA/C Sawyer; 10 AA/R Elliot; 11 AA/C Sawyer; 12 AA/E Rooney; 13 AA/S McBride; 14 AA/E Rooney; 15 AA/C Sawyer; 16/7 AA/R Elliot; 18 AA/P Kenward; 19 AA/D Corrance; 20/1 AA/D Corrance; 22 AA/D Corrance; 23 AA/D Corrance; 24 AA/R Elliot; 25 AA/D Corrance; 26 AA/C Sawyer; 26/7 AA/C Sawyer; 28 AA; 29 AA/S McBride; 30/1 AA/P Kenward; 32 AA/P Kenward; 33 AA/C Sawyer; 34 AA/D Pollack; 35 AA/C Sawyer; 36 AA/S McBride; 37 AA/C Sawyer; 38/9 AA/E Rooney; 40 AA/P Kenward; 41 AA/C Sawyer; 42/3 AA/S McBride; 44 AA/C Sawyer; 45 AA/C Sawyer; 46 AA/S McBride; 47 AA/C Sawyer; 48/9 AA/P Kenward; 49 AA/C Sawyer; 50/1 AA/C Sawyer; 52 AA/S McBride; 53 AA/C Sawyer; 54 AA/ S McBride; 55 AA/C Sawyer; 56/7 AA/C Sawyer; 58 AA/D Corrance; 59 AA/ S McBride; 60 AA/C Sawyer; 61 AA/C Sawyer; 62 AA/C Sawyer; 63 AA/ S McBride; 64/5 AA/R Elliot; 65 AA/C Sawyer; 66 AA/ P Kenward; 67 AA/C Sawyer; 68 AA/E Rooney; 69 AA/S McBride; 70 AA/C Sawyer; 71 AA/S McBride; 72 AA/C Sawyer; 73 AA/S McBride; 74/5 AA/S McBride; 76 AA/S McBride; 77 AA/P Kenward; 78/9 AA/S McBride; 80 AA/C Sawyer; 81 AA/C Sawyer; 82/3 AA/C Sawyer; 84 AA/S McBride; 85 AA/S McBride; 86/7 AA/C Sawyer; 88 AA/R Elliot; 89 AA/C Sawyer; 90 AA/C Sawyer; 91 AA/C Sawyer; 92/3 AA/S McBride; 94 AA/C Sawyer; 94/5 AA/S McBride.

Every effort has been made to trace the copyright holders, and we apologise in advance for any accidental errors. We would be happy to apply the corrections in the following edition of this publication.